Hawaiian

AMERICAN

REGIONAL COOKING
LIBRARY
Culture, Tradition,
and History

African American

American Indian

Amish and Mennonite

California

Hawaiian

Louisiana

Mexican American

Mid–Atlantic

Midwest

New England

Northwest

Southern Appalachia

Southern

Texas

Thanksgiving

Hawaiian

Mason Crest Publishers

Philadelphia

Mason Crest Publishers Inc.
370 Reed Road
Broomall, Pennsylvania 19008
(866) MCP-BOOK (toll free)
www.masoncrest.com

First printing
1 2 3 4 5 6 7 8 9 10

Library of Congress Cataloging-in-Publication Data

Hawaiian / compiled by Joyce Libal ; recipes by Patricia Therrien.
     p. cm.—(American regional cooking library)
 Includes bibliographical references and index.
 ISBN 1-59084-614-1
 1. Cookery, Hawaiian—Juvenile literature. I. Libal, Joyce. II. Therrien, Patricia. III. Series.
 TX724.5.H3H28 2005
  741.59969—dc22
                                    2004007771
Compiled by Joyce Libal.
Recipes by Patricia Therrien.

Produced by Harding House Publishing Services, Inc., Vestal, New York.
Interior design by Dianne Hodack.
Cover design by Michelle Bouch.
Printed and bound in the Hashemite Kingdom of Jordan.

Contents

Introduction   6–7

Hawaiian Culture, History, and Traditions   8–11

Before You Cook

  · safety tips   12–13

  · metric conversion table   14

  · useful tools   15–16

  · cooking glossary   16–17

  · special Hawaiian flavors   18

Hawaiian Recipes   20–65

Further Reading   66

For More Information   67

Index   68–69

Biographies   70

Picture Credits   71

Introduction
by the Culinary Institute of America

Cooking is a dynamic profession, one that presents some of the greatest challenges and offers some of the greatest rewards. Since 1946, the Culinary Institute of America has provided aspiring and seasoned food service professionals with the knowledge and skills needed to become leaders and innovators in this industry.

Here at the CIA, we teach our students the fundamental culinary techniques they need to build a sound foundation for their food service careers. There is always another level of perfection for them to achieve and another skill to master. Our rigorous curriculum provides them with a springboard to continued growth and success.

Food is far more than simply sustenance or the source of energy to fuel you and your family through life's daily regimen. It conjures memories throughout life, summoning up the smell, taste, and flavor of simpler times. Cooking is more than an art and a science; it provides family history. Food prepared with care epitomizes the love, devotion, and culinary delights that you offer to your friends and family.

A cuisine provides a way to express and establish customs—the way a food should taste and the flavors and aromas associated with that food. Cuisines are more than just a collection of ingredients, cooking utensils, and dishes from a geographic location; they are elements that are critical to establishing a culinary identity.

When you can accurately read a recipe, you can trace a variety of influences by observing which ingredients are selected and also by noting the technique that is used. If you research the historical origins of a recipe, you may find ingredients that traveled from East to West or from the New World to the Old. Traditional methods of cooking a dish may have changed with the times or to meet special challenges.

The history of cooking illustrates the significance of innovation and the trading or sharing of ingredients and tools between societies. Although the various cooking vessels over the years have changed, the basic cooking methods have remained the same. Through adaptation, a recipe created years ago in a remote corner of the world could today be recognized by many throughout the globe.

When observing the customs of different societies, it becomes apparent that food brings people together. It is the common thread that we share and that we value. Regardless of the occasion, food is present to celebrate and to comfort. Through food we can experience other cultures and lands, learning the significance of particular ingredients and cooking techniques.

As you begin your journey through the culinary arts, keep in mind the power that food and cuisine holds. When passed from generation to generation, family heritage and traditions remain strong. Become familiar with the dishes your family has enjoyed through the years and play a role in keeping them alive. Don't be afraid to embellish recipes along the way – creativity is what cooking is all about.

Hawaiian Culture, History, and Traditions

Hawaii (*Hawai'i* in Hawaiian spelling), our most recent state and the only one to grow coffee and chocolate, was admitted to the Union in 1959. Polynesians were its first inhabitants, arriving approximately 1500 years ago. Today, more than a million people live in this state that has two official languages (English and Hawaiian).

The Polynesians brought many plants to Hawaii, including breadfruit and taro, which became staple foods. Bananas, coconuts, and sugar cane also came with the Polynesians as did pigs, another important food source.

James Cook is the European who is credited with having discovered the Islands in 1778. The inhabitants, who believed him to be a god called Lono, welcomed him.

All of the Islands were united under Kamehameha I in 1810, after he initiated and won a war against the other rulers.

By 1819, whaling ships arrived, and whaling was conducted near the Islands for several decades.

American missionaries came to the Hawaiian Islands in 1820 and immediately set about altering the culture. For example, the hula had been used for generations as a means of remembering stories and passing them on to others. When missionaries saw the hula, however, they banned it. To the credit of missionaries, they did create a written language for Hawaiian, condoned inter-racial marriage, and started schools, but people were soon forbidden to speak Hawaiian there.

During the reign of King David Kalakaua, an effort was made to restore some of the Hawaiian heritage. King Kalakaua said, "Hula is the language of the heart and therefore the heartbeat of the Hawaiian people." Unfortunately, even though many good cultural things took place during King Kalakaua's reign, when threatened with force, he signed a document that became known as the "Bayonet Constitution." This document effectively destroyed the power of the monarchy and made it legal for foreigners to vote.

Since 1850, foreigners had been able to own land on the Islands. Plantations with crops such as pineapples, cotton, tobacco, and sugar cane, had been developed. In the

An open-air market in Hilo, Hawaii.

1890s, some of the large plantations began to be divided into smaller farms and dairies. During that time, the Kingdom of Hawaii was an independent country. In 1893, the United States Congress imposed a large tariff on Hawaiian sugar. The plantation owners wanted more control in Hawaii and to find a way to reduce their tariffs, so they enlisted the support of United States troops in their plan to destroy the monarchy. Queen Liliu'okalani, who was the monarch at that time, was threatened and coerced into relinquishing her throne. The "Committee of Safety" (composed of Europeans and Americans) took control, and soon a man named Sanford Dole became president.

It wasn't until 1993 that the United States Congress passed a Joint Resolution apologizing for its part in the illegal overthrow of the Hawaiian monarchy.

Hawaii became a United States territory in 1900. In the 1920s and '30s, the term "local food" was used to categorize the East-West Pacific blend of food traditions in Hawaii. Poi was included under this heading, as was food served with soy sauce and sesame oil. Meat and rice with gravy were also included. Today, a new term, "Hawaiian regional cuisine," is used to describe the way cooking has evolved on the Islands. This is a blend of Asian cooking traditions, traditions from the United States mainland, and local Hawaiian products and food culture. Fresh Hawaiian fruits like mangoes and guava are made into sauces that pair beautifully with swordfish and tuna and scores of other fish. Of course, countless other foods are also included, many of which you'll encounter in the recipes included here. It's time to share in the distinctive and delicious cuisine of Hawaii.

Before you cook...

If you haven't done much cooking before, you may find recipe books a little confusing. Certain words and terms can seem unfamiliar. You may find the measurements difficult to understand. What appears to be an easy or familiar dish may contain ingredients you've never heard of before. You might not understand what utensil the recipe calls for you to use, or you might not be sure what the recipe is asking you to do.

Reading the pages in this section before you get started may help you understand the directions better so that your cooking goes more smoothly. You can also refer back to these pages whenever you run into questions.

Safety Tips

Cooking involves handling very hot and very sharp objects, so being careful is common sense. What's more, you want to be certain that anything you plan on putting in your mouth is safe to eat. If you follow these easy tips, you should find that cooking can be both fun and safe.

Before you cook...

- Always wash your hands before and after handling food. This is particularly important after you handle raw meats, poultry, and eggs, as bacteria called salmonella can live on these uncooked foods. You can't see or smell salmonella, but these germs can make you or anyone who swallows them very sick.
- Make a habit of using potholders or oven mitts whenever you handle pots and pans from the oven or microwave.
- Always set pots, pans, and knives with their handles away from counter edges. This way you won't risk catching your sleeves on them—and any younger children in the house won't be in danger of grabbing something hot or sharp.
- Don't leave perishable food sitting out of the refrigerator for more than an hour or two.
- Wash all raw fruits and vegetables to remove dirt and chemicals.
- Use a cutting board when chopping vegetables or fruit, and always cut away from yourself.
- Don't overheat grease or oil—but if grease or oil does catch fire, don't try to extinguish the flames with water. Instead, throw baking soda or salt on the fire to put it out. Turn all stove burners off.
- If you burn yourself, immediately put the burn under cold water, as this will prevent the burn from becoming more painful.
- Never put metal dishes or utensils in the microwave. Use only microwave-proof dishes.
- Wash cutting boards and knives thoroughly after cutting meat, fish or poultry — especially when raw and before using the same tools to prepare other foods such as vegetables and cheese. This will prevent the spread of bacteria such as salmonella.
- Keep your hands away from any moving parts of appliances, such as mixers.
- Unplug any appliance, such as a mixer, blender, or food processor before assembling for use or disassembling after use.

Metric Conversion Table

Most cooks in the United States use measuring containers based on an eight-ounce cup, a teaspoon, and a tablespoon. Meanwhile, cooks in Canada and Europe are more apt to use metric measurements. The recipes in this book use cups, teaspoons, and tablespoons—but you can convert these measurements to metric by using the table below.

Temperature
To convert Fahrenheit degrees to Celsius, subtract 32 and multiply by .56.

212ºF = 100ºC
(this is the boiling point of water)
250ºF = 110ºC
275ºF = 135ºC
300ºF = 150ºC
325ºF = 160ºC
350ºF = 180ºC
375ºF = 190ºC
400ºF = 200ºC

Liquid Measurements
1 teaspoon = 5 milliliters
1 tablespoon = 15 milliliters
1 fluid ounce = 30 milliliters
1 cup = 240 milliliters
1 pint = 480 milliliters
1 quart = 0.95 liters
1 gallon = 3.8 liters

Measurements of Mass or Weight
1 ounce = 28 grams
8 ounces = 227 grams
1 pound (16 ounces) = 0.45 kilograms
2.2 pounds = 1 kilogram

Measurements of Length
¼ inch = 0.6 centimeters
½ inch = 1.25 centimeters
1 inch = 2.5 centimeters

Pan Sizes

Baking pans are usually made in standard sizes. The pans used in the United States are roughly equivalent to the following metric pans:

9-inch cake pan = 23-centimeter pan
11x7-inch baking pan = 28x18-centimeter baking pan
13x9-inch baking pan = 32.5x23-centimeter baking pan
9x5-inch loaf pan = 23x13-centimeter loaf pan
2-quart casserole = 2-liter casserole

Useful Tools, Utensils, Dishes

basting brush

blender

candy thermometer

electric mixer

flour sifter

garlic press

long-handled slotted spoon

rubber spatula

vegetable shredder

wire whisk

wok

Cooking Glossary

cut Mix solid shortening or butter into flour, usually by using a pastry blender or two knives and making short, chopping strokes until the mixture looks like small pellets.

dash A very small amount, just a couple of shakes or drops.

deep fry To fry a food completely immersed in hot cooking oil or melted shortening so that all sides cook evenly and at the same time.

dice Cut into small cubes or pieces.

dollop A small mound, about 1 or 2 tablespoons.

fillet Thin strips of boneless fish or meat.

fold Gently combine a lighter substance with a heavier batter by spooning the lighter mixture through the heavier one without using strong beating strokes.

knead To work dough with the hands, lifting the far edge, placing it upon the rest, and pushing with the heal of the hands.

marinade Brine or other liquid in which fish or meat is soaked to enhance flavor.

minced Cut into very small pieces.

sauté Fry in a skillet or wok over high heat while stirring.

set When a food preparation has completed the thickening process and can be sliced.

simmer Gently boiling, so that the surface of the liquid just ripples gently.

steam To cook over just a small amount of boiling water.

toss Turn food over quickly and lightly so that it is evenly covered with a liquid or powder.

whisk Stir briskly with a wire whisk.

Special Hawaiian Flavors

fish sauce

fresh ginger

garlic

macadamia nuts

mango

soy sauce

teriyaki sauce

vanilla

Hawaiian Recipes

Mango Bread

The unique flavors of mangoes and macadamia nuts make this bread delicious any time of the day.

Preheat oven to 350° Fahrenheit.

Ingredients:

2 cups flour
1½ cups sugar
2 teaspoons baking soda
1 teaspoon cloves
1 teaspoon allspice
½ teaspoon salt
3 eggs
½ cup cooking oil
½ cup melted butter
2 cups mangoes (partly mashed and partly diced)
(see "Tip")
½ cup chopped macadamia nuts

Cooking utensils you'll need:
measuring cups
measuring spoons
2 mixing bowls
electric mixer
loaf pan

Directions:

Grease and lightly flour the loaf pan, and set it aside. Put the flour in one of the mixing bowls. Stir in the sugar, baking soda, cloves, allspice, and salt, and set it aside. Use the electric mixer to beat the eggs in the second bowl. Beat in oil and melted butter, and continue beating for 2 minutes at medium speed. Pour the egg mixture into the flour mixture, and stir just until well combined. Fold in mango and chopped nuts, pour into the prepared pan, and bake for 45 to 55 minutes.

manako' (mah nah KOH)—mango

Tip:

Mangoes have become a familiar sight at grocery stores throughout North America. If you haven't tried them yet, stop denying yourself this sweet treat. Don't judge mangoes by their color. Instead, purchase mangoes that are just beginning to soften, or allow them to soften a bit at room temperature before peeling. You can usually slice the peeled mango in half along one side of the flat seed, and then cut that section into smaller pieces. The riper the mango, the more the juice flows as you peel and slice it. If it becomes too ripe, you may want use it in a smoothie. Just rub and squeeze the unpeeled fruit. Then cut a slice off the stem end, hold the fruit over a blender container, and squeeze as much juice out of it as possible. Add a banana, strawberries, or any other fruit that you like, some yogurt, and a few ice cubes. Blend until smooth, and serve over more ice for a nutritious and refreshing drink.

Hawaiian Food History

People have been eating mangoes for over 6,000 years, and today more than 17 million metric tons of them are consumed annually. You may have thought that all mangoes are alike, but they actually come in more than fifty different varieties and can be many shades of green, yellow, orange, pink, purple, and red. This healthy food is low in fat and calories, yet contains loads of vitamins, minerals, antioxidants, and fiber. It also contains a unique enzyme that aids digestion.

Macadamia nuts are grown on the Hawaiian Islands and exported around the world. You can purchase them plain or roasted and salted. They are creamy and delicious straight from the can, or use them to make cookies, candies, and other foods.

Many other fruits are grown in Hawaii, including papaya, breadfruit, and pomelo.

Malasadas

This special Hawaiian treat has Portuguese roots. The holeless doughnut is popular at family and community gatherings.

Ingredients:

¼ cup very warm water
1 package active dry yeast
6 cups flour
½ cup plus 1 teaspoon sugar
½ teaspoon salt
6 eggs
¼ cup melted butter or margarine
1 cup water
1 cup evaporated milk
1 quart (4 cups) vegetable oil
extra sugar to coat cooked malasadas

Cooking utensils you'll need:
measuring cups
measuring spoons
1 small bowl
2 large mixing bowls
wire whisk
clean kitchen towel
candy thermometer
deep-sided pan for frying
long-handled slotted spoon
paper bag

Directions:

Put the very warm water in the small bowl, sprinkle the yeast over it, and stir to dissolve. Add 1 teaspoon sugar, stir again, and set it aside. Put the flour in one of the large mixing bowls, and stir in the remaining ½ cup sugar and the salt. *Whisk* the eggs in the remaining mixing bowl. Make a depression in the center of the flour, and pour the eggs into it. Add the melted butter, 1 cup of water, and evaporated milk. Stir until well blended. When the dough is soft, cover the bowl with a towel, and set it aside in a warm spot in your kitchen until the dough has doubled in size. Then, without punching it down, carefully turn the dough upside down in the bowl, cover it again, and set it aside to rise a second time.

Pour the oil into the deep-sided pan, attach the thermometer, and heat the oil to 375º. Put spoonfuls of dough onto the slotted spoon and lower them into the hot oil. Fry, turning them as necessary, until they are browned. (Make just one malasada first, and eat it while it is still warm to test for doneness, see "Tips.") Cook the malasadas in batches. Put some sugar into a bag, place hot malasadas in the bag, and shake to coat them well. Enjoy them while they are still warm.

Tips:

If the first malasada is doughy in the center, reduce the heat so the remaining ones will cook more slowly.

You can add cinnamon or nutmeg to the sugar in the paper bag. This is not the traditional Hawaiian way to make them, but they are delicious with these spices.

Hawaiian Coleslaw

Make this crunchy pineapple-laced slaw for your next "lu'au."

Ingredients:

4 cups shredded cabbage
½ cup mayonnaise
1 tablespoon milk
1 cup crushed pineapple
1 tablespoon vinegar

½ teaspoon sugar
¼ teaspoon salt
dash of pepper
dash of paprika

Cooking utensils you'll need:
measuring cups
measuring spoons
vegetable shredder
2 mixing bowls

Directions:

Put the shredded cabbage in one bowl, and set it aside. Mix the mayonnaise and milk in the second bowl. Drain the crushed pineapple, save the juice for another purpose, and pour the pineapple into the mayonnaise/milk mixture. Stir in the remaining ingredients, pour it over the cabbage, and *toss.*

Hawaiian Food History

Even if you've never been to the Hawaiian Islands, you probably have a mental image of a luau. Imagine a warm night filled with family and friends, traditional Hawaiian music and dancers, roast pig and a multitude of other traditional foods, fire rising into the sky, and ocean waves lapping against the beach. This is one of the cultural traditions in Hawaii that every visitor longs to experience.

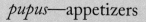

pupus—appetizers

Kamaboko Salad

Look for kamaboko (a loaf or cake of steamed or pureed fish) in Asian markets. Although it is usually white, kamaboko may contain food coloring. Sometimes kamaboko is purchased attached to a board. This unusual food can be used to make soups and other hot dishes as well as the cold dish described here.

Ingredients:

4 ounces spaghetti noodles
1 piece kamaboko
1 cup chopped celery (or 1 cup shredded cabbage)
1 tablespoon chopped green onion
mayonnaise
salt and pepper to taste
salad greens

Cooking utensils you'll need:
measuring cup
mixing bowl

Directions:

Cook the spaghetti according to package directions, drain, place in the mixing bowl, and sprinkle with a little salt. Cut the kamaboko into thin strips, and then cut them again in the opposite direction. Mix the kamaboko with the spaghetti. Mix in the celery and green onion. Add the desired amount of mayonnaise, season to taste with salt and pepper, and serve on a bed of salad greens.

Hawaiian Tradition

Visitors to Hawaii are sometimes presented with leis, a symbol of friend-ship when arriving or leaving the Islands. Traditionally, flower leis were used to celebrate special occasions and to mark the memorable moments of an individual's life. Happy occasions such as birthdays and marriage and sadder ones such as funerals all warranted these special creations. Each type of flower had a special meaning. Some leis weren't made of flowers at all. Beads, feathers, and other objects were sometimes used to make leis that were longer lasting than those made of flowers.

Gingered Carrots

These sweet and spicy carrots really perk up a meal.

Ingredients:

5 carrots, sliced
¼ cup orange juice
1 tablespoon sugar
¼ teaspoon dry ginger
¼ teaspoon salt
1 teaspoon cornstarch

Cooking utensils you'll need:
measuring cup
measuring spoons
saucepan
bowl

Directions:

Put the carrots in the saucepan, cover them with water, add a couple shakes of salt, and *simmer* until tender (about 15 to 20 minutes). Drain the carrots, put them in a bowl, and set them aside. Mix the remaining ingredients in the saucepan, and cook over medium heat until it begins to thicken. Stir in the carrots, heat just until the carrots are hot, and serve.

Hawaiian Tradition

In Hawaiian society the concept of family was broad enough to extend beyond the immediate family to other people who were loved. Elders were highly respected, and children were treasured. Children were often cared for by more people than just their parents or even grandparents. Hanai was a sort of unofficial adoption that was part of Hawaiian culture. According to this custom, a child might be offered by his parents to a family member (such as a grandparent) or a special friend (perhaps someone who did not have a child of her own). This may sound strange when taken out of the context of the Hawaiian culture. But it was a way of demonstrating the immensity of people's love and respect for one another. It also made family and friendship bonds even stronger.

mahalo—thank you

Taro root.

Poi Cakes

Poi is made by cooking and pounding taro corms (underground stems or tubers) into a sticky sort of paste. Like thrifty cooks in other parts of North America, Hawaiian homemakers often make use of leftover ingredients like mashed potatoes and poi. These vegetable patties may have first been made with either potatoes or mashed taro in the 1930s or '40s. Look for poi in 8-ounce containers or 4-ounce tubes in the specialty-foods section of your supermarket.

Preheat oven to 350° Fahrenheit.

Ingredients:

2 tablespoons butter
½ cup **minced** onion
3 tablespoons minced parsley
1 cup poi
1 cup mashed potatoes
dash of salt
3 tablespoons flour
additional butter (see "Directions")

Cooking utensils you'll need:
measuring cups
measuring spoons
skillet
cookie sheet

Directions:

Grease the cookie sheet, and set it aside. Melt 2 tablespoons butter in the skillet, and stir in onion and parsley. Sauté until onion is tender. Stir in the poi. Gradually add the mashed potatoes, salt, and flour. When the mixture is cool enough to handle, use your hands to form it into small patties, and place them on the cookie sheet. Make a small depression on top of each patty, and set about ¼ teaspoon of butter in it. Bake for 20 minute (or until the outside of the patties are crispy and a golden color). Serve hot.

Tip:

You can also form the potato mixture into small balls and deep-fry them. To do this, pour about 3 or 4 inches of cooking oil into a deep-sided pan. Attach a candy thermometer to the pan, and heat the oil to 350°. Use a long-handled slotted spoon to carefully lower the balls into the hot oil, and fry until golden brown.

Taro plants.

Hawaiian Food Tradition

Hawaiians may have been eating poi as long ago as A.D. 450, but the taro plant, from which poi is made, was grown elsewhere as early as 23 B.C., making it one of the oldest cultivated foods. Although women were allowed to grow other foods, at first only men were allowed to grow and harvest taro and pound the corms into poi. The Polynesians were the ones who brought this important food to the Hawaiian Islands. Of all foods, taro was thought to possess the greatest life force. According to Hawaiian mythology, father sky and mother earth (or the daughter of mother earth depending upon the source of the legend) had a first child that was stillborn. They named this baby Haloanaka (which means quivering long stalk) before burying him. The first taro plant grew from Haloanaka's grave. Later, father sky and mother earth had another son, named Haloa, and he became the father of the Hawaiian people. In this way, taro was thought to be the older brother of man and was, therefore, highly revered in the Hawaiian culture. Many customs developed concerning poi's production and consumption. People were not to speak in angry tones or to argue with one another when poi was being served. Not surprisingly, fingers were the first utensils used to eat poi.

There are many varieties of the taro plant. In fact, Hawaiians might have been growing as many as 200 different varieties a century before Europeans arrived on the Islands! Poi becomes increasingly sour tasting as it ages. Day-old poi, three-day poi, etc. are terms used to describe the degree of sourness that has developed.

ono—taste good ("It's ono poi.")

Pipi Kaula

Make this Hawaiian version of beef jerky at home in the oven.

Ingredients:

2 pounds flank steak
¾ cup soy sauce
2 tablespoons Hawaiian salt (see "Tip")
1½ tablespoons sugar
1 piece of ginger, **minced**
1 red chili pepper, crushed
1 garlic clove

Cooking utensils you'll need:
measuring cup
measuring spoons
mixing bowl
garlic press
plastic wrap
baking rack
cookie sheet

Directions:

Wash the meat, pat it dry with paper towels, and cut it into 1 1/3-inch wide slices. Pour the soy sauce into the mixing bowl. Stir in the remaining ingredients, using the garlic press to press the garlic. (If you don't have a garlic press, mince the garlic.) Place the sliced meat into the liquid, cover with plastic wrap, and place in the refrigerator overnight.

Preheat oven to 175° Fahrenheit. Put the baking rack on the cookie sheet, place the meat slices on the rack, and bake for approximately 7 hours. Store dried meat in the refrigerator.

Hawaiian Food History

Suprisingly, the biggest cattle ranch in America is located in the Hawaiian Islands. Missionaries were probably the first ones to bring cows to Hawaii.

Tip:

Hawaiian salt is different from table salt in both taste and appearance. This sea salt was one of the first commodities traded to foreigners during the beginning of the nineteenth century. It was extracted from the sea in "salt pans" that were constructed in special areas reserved for this purpose. The largest pans in the 1800s were in Kawaihae on the island of Hawaii. Hawaiian salt is available through mail-order sources on the Internet, or you may substitute Kosher salt when using the recipes in this book.

Loco Moco

The next time you get hungry for a hamburger, try this exclusive Hawaiian version on for size.

Ingredients:

1 pound lean ground beef (see "Tips")
5 eggs
2 tablespoons ketchup
½ teaspoon salt
½ teaspoon pepper
2 tablespoons cooking oil
4 cups cooked rice
1 cup prepared gravy (leftover from another meal or canned)

Cooking utensils you'll need:
measuring spoons
mixing bowl
saucepan
2 skillets
ice cream scoop

Directions:

Cook rice according to package directions. Put the ground beef into the mixing bowl, and stir in one egg. Mix in the ketchup, salt, and pepper. Use your hands to form the mixture into 4 hamburger patties, and fry them until cooked through, flipping them over once to brown each side. Meanwhile, fry 4 eggs in the cooking oil. To serve, use the ice cream scoop to place a mound of rice on each plate, set a hamburger on the rice, pour gravy over it, and place an egg on top.

Tips:

Although this dish is usually served with the eggs fried "sunny-side-up," you can substitute poached eggs.

Use ground pork, turkey, or chicken instead of beef in this dish. You can also use sausage, teriyaki beef or chicken, shrimp, oysters, or mahi-mahi fish.

Hawaiian Food History

This regional favorite had its beginnings in 1949 in a town called Hilo on the big island of Hawaii. It all started when teens from a local athletic club began hanging out at the Lincoln Grill, a local restaurant. The kids liked to play the jukebox and pin ball machines, and that didn't leave much cash left over for food. They nominated a boy, nicknamed "Crazy" because of his antics when playing football, to ask the owners if they could develop an inexpensive yet filling food that would taste great. The first loco mocos cost only .25 but were minus the egg, which was added at a later date. It was soon one of the most requested foods served, and the teens named it for their friend, using loco, the Spanish word for "crazy." "Moco" was added later because it rhymed with loco. The Lincoln Grill closed in the 1960s, but the loco moco is now served throughout the Hawaiian Islands.

brok' da mout—it tastes good

Lumpia and Sauce

Treat your family to these Hawaiian-style "egg rolls." Descendants from many different ethnic groups now call the Hawaiian Islands home, including people from the Philippines, who are responsible for this culinary delight.

Ingredients:

one 8-ounce can water chestnuts
1 large onion, minced
5 garlic cloves
1 pound lean ground beef
two 10-ounce packages frozen chop suey vegetables
1⅛ teaspoon salt
¼ teaspoon pepper
1 tablespoon patis (see "Tips")
2 tablespoons flour
¼ cup water
40 lumpia wrappers (see "Tips")
cooking oil
¼ cup vinegar

Water chestnuts

Cooking utensils you'll need:
measuring spoons
garlic press
2 small bowls
skillet
candy thermometer
deep sided pan
long-handled slotted spoon

Directions:

Cut the water chestnuts into thin slices, and set them aside. Place beef and onion in skillet. Use the garlic press to press 2 garlic cloves over the meat. (If you don't have a garlic press, mince the garlic.) Cook over medium heat until meat is cooked through, and drain off the excess fat. Stir in the water chestnuts, chop suey vegetables, 1 teaspoon of the salt, pepper, and patis, and cook 2 minutes. Mix the flour and water, and set it aside. Take a lumpia wrapper, place a couple tablespoons of cooled meat filling on the wrapper, fold it like an envelope, and use the flour/water mixture like a paste to help seal it. Repeat with the remaining wrappers and filling. Pour a couple inches of cooking oil into the deep-sided pan, attach the candy thermometer, place it over medium heat, and bring the oil to 375° Fahrenheit. Place a lumpia on the slotted spoon, carefully lower it into the hot oil, and fry until golden brown on all sides. Fry several lumpia at a time, and drain on paper towels. Meanwhile, pour the vinegar in the remaining bowl. Use the garlic press to press the remaining 3 garlic cloves into it, and stir in the remaining ⅛ teaspoon salt. Serve this dipping sauce with the hot lumpia.

Tips:

Lumpia wrappers, made of flour, eggs, and water, are very thin. If you are not able to locate them in your supermarket, substitute traditional egg roll wrappers.

Patis was introduced to the Hawaiian Islands by people from the Philippines. It is a thin sauce made from salted and fermented fish. It only takes a small amount of this pungent ingredient to impart a unique flavor to food.

Hawaiian Food History

In the nineteenth and twentieth centuries, waves of laborers were brought in from many countries, including Japan, China, Thailand, Portugal, Samoa, Puerto Rico, Korea, and Vietnam. All these people brought their food traditions with them. Many of them kept the uniqueness of their ethnic cuisine because plantation owners housed different ethnic groups in separate locations.

Kalua Pig

You don't need to dig up your yard to cook pork roast for your luau. Instead, just follow these simple directions.

Preheat oven to 350° Fahrenheit.

Ingredients:

4 to 5 pound pork roast
2½ tablespoons Hawaiian salt (see "Tip" on page 35)
2 tablespoons liquid smoke
1 banana leaf (substitute 4 or 5 whole, unpeeled bananas)
4 to 6 ti leaves (substitute aluminum foil)

Cooking utensils you'll need:
measuring spoons
fork
roasting pan

Directions:

Wash but do not peel the bananas, and set them aside. Wash the roast, pat it dry with paper towels, and remove any excess fat. Use the fork to pierce the meat in many places. (The goal is to make many holes to help flavors enter the meat.) Use your hands to rub the salt and liquid smoke into the roast. Place the meat in the roasting pan, and put the bananas on top. Cover the roast and bananas with aluminum foil, sealing it well along the edges of the pan. (If you are using a banana leaf instead of the bananas, wrap the roast in the leaf. If you have ti leaves, remove any stiff ribs, and wrap the ti leaves around the banana leaf. Use string to securely tie the leaves around the meat.) Bake for 45 minutes for each pound of meat. (For example, bake a 4 pound roast for 3 hours; bake a 5 pound roast for 3 hours and 45 minutes.) Pull the roast into shreds before serving.

Hawaiian Food History and Tradition

The Polynesians brought pigs to the Hawaiian Islands. Kalua pig (shredded pork), cooked using the "imu method," is the most common food served at Hawaiian luaus. The imu method is something like a pit barbecue. The cooking pit is dug in the ground, and hot rocks are placed under and around the pig. The cooking pig is covered with ti leaves (a member of the agave family) and banana leaves. Then burlap is placed upon the leaves, and earth is placed upon the burlap. All of this is a big undertaking, even in Hawaii, and many recipes have been developed to make it easier to cook kalua pig.

Hawaiian Food History and Tradition

The Chinese were among many ethnic groups who came to the Islands to work on large plantations.

Chicken Long Rice

Immigrants from China contributed this now-traditional food to the Hawaiian luau.

Ingredients:

3 pounds boneless and skinless chicken pieces
6 tablespoons soy sauce
1 tablespoon sesame oil
2 tablespoons **minced** fresh ginger
1½ teaspoons sugar
dash pepper
3 garlic cloves

10 ounces long rice noodles
 (cellophane noodles)
2 tablespoons cooking oil
8 ounces sliced mushrooms
4 chopped green onions
8 ounces chicken broth
1 sliced red pepper as garnish

Directions:

Wash the meat, pat it dry with paper towels, cut it into strips or small pieces, and set it aside. Put 2 tablespoons of the soy sauce in one of the mixing bowls. Stir in sesame oil, minced ginger, sugar, and pepper. Use the garlic press to press the garlic over the mixture. (If you don't have a garlic press, mince the garlic.) Stir again, add the chicken, cover the bowl with plastic wrap, and refrigerate for 1 hour.

After the chicken has been in the refrigerator for 30 minutes, put the noodles in the second mixing bowl, cover with cold water, and allow them to soak. After they have soaked for 30 minutes, drain the chicken, and begin heating the wok over high heat. Pour the cooking oil into the wok, add the chicken pieces, stir and fry until it is no longer pink, and then turn the heat down to medium. Stir in the mushrooms and green onions. Add the noodles, chicken broth, and remaining 4 tablespoons of soy sauce. Continue to stir-fry until everything is hot (about 3 minutes), being careful not to overcook the noodles. Serve hot; garnish with sliced red pepper if desired.

Char Siu Bao

There are several steps to creating these steamed pockets of pork, but making them can be a fun family activity.

Ingredients:

Part 1:
2 to 3 pounds pork
½ cup soy sauce
½ cup dry cooking sherry
¾ cup hoisin sauce (see "Tips")
⅓ cup honey
1 tablespoon sugar
additional honey (optional)

Part 2:
¾ cup prepared pork (char siu)
2 teaspoons flour
2 teaspoons cornstarch
¼ cup water
1 teaspoon sesame oil
3 tablespoons chopped green onions
2 ½ tablespoons sugar
4 teaspoons soy sauce
⅛ teaspoon salt

Part 3:
1 cup very warm water
1 package active dry yeast
¼ cup sugar
3½ cups flour
1 tablespoon shortening

Cooking utensils you'll need:
measuring cups
measuring spoons
large mixing bowl
plastic wrap
baking rack
roasting pan (large enough to accommodate baking rack)
basting brush
small bowl
wok or skillet
wooden cutting board (or other flat surface)
clean towel
waxed paper
covered deep-sided pan
rack that fits within covered pan

Directions:

Part 1: Wash the meat, pat it dry with paper towels, cut it into 2-inch by 5-inch strips, and set it aside. Pour ½ cup soy sauce into the large mixing bowl, stir in the sherry, hoisin sauce, honey, and 1 tablespoon sugar. Add the meat, cover with plastic wrap, and refrigerate for at least 2 hours (overnight is even better).

Preheat oven to 450º Fahrenheit. Put the rack in the roasting pan and add hot water until it is almost touching the rack. Drain the meat and save the *marinade*, place the pork strips on the rack, and bake for 10 minutes. Lower oven temperature to 325º Fahrenheit. Bake for 30 to 40 additional minutes, turning the meat and basting with the marinade every 10 minutes. Ten minutes before baking is complete, brush the meat with honey, if desired. Cut the pork into bite size pieces, and set them aside.

Part 2: Mix together 2 teaspoons flour, cornstarch, and ¼ cup water in the small bowl, and set aside. Put the sesame oil into a hot wok, add the prepared pork, and stir-fry for 30 seconds. Add the onions, 2½ tablespoons sugar, 4 teaspoons soy sauce, salt, and flour/water mixture. Continue stir-frying until the liquid thickens, and cools. This completes the char siu filling.

Part 3: Put ⅓ cup of very warm water in a small bowl. Sprinkle the yeast over it, stir to dissolve, stir in 2 tablespoons sugar and ½ cup flour, and set aside. Put 3 cups flour into the large mixing bowl. *Cut* in the 1 tablespoon shortening. Pour the yeast mixture and remaining ⅔ cup water into the flour mixture, and stir well. Sprinkle some flour on the wooden board or another flat surface, and *knead* dough until it is smooth and elastic. (Add more flour as necessary while kneading, but be careful not to add too much as it can make the dough stiff and dry.) Grease the bowl with a little oil, put the dough into it, put a little oil on the surface of the dough, cover the bowl with a towel, and let it sit in a warm spot in your kitchen for about an hour.

Rub a little cooking oil on the palms of your hands. Using your hands, divide the dough into 18 equal-sized pieces. Working with one piece of dough at a time, flatten the dough with your hand, place 1 tablespoon of char siu filling in the center, pull the edges of the dough to the center, and pinch the edges together to fill the char siu bao. Set it on a piece of waxed paper, repeat with the remaining ingredients, and let the char siu bao rest for 20 minutes. Place the rack in the deep-sided pan, and put water into the pan to beneath the rack. Place char siu bao on the rack, cover, and *steam* for about 18 minutes.

Tips:

Hoisin sauce is often used for poultry, meat, and shellfish dishes in Chinese cooking. This rather thick mixture of soybeans, chile peppers, and garlic is a red/brown color and imparts a sweet and spicy flavor to foods. Bottled hoisin sauce will last indefinitely in your refrigerator. If you purchase canned hoisin sauce, transfer the unused portion to a glass jar before refrigerating. You can find this popular ingredient in most supermarkets and in Asian markets.

The char siu pork in this recipe can also be used to make the Quick-Fried Rice on page 51.

Lomi Lomi

Cooking utensils you'll need:
mixing bowl
plastic wrap

Lomi means massage *in Hawaiian, and you'll see how that name applies to this recipe when you read the directions below. Traditionally, this luau appetizer is made of raw, salted fish, but smoked salmon is used in this recipe.*

Ingredients:

8 ounces smoked salmon **fillet** *(also called lox)*
4 tomatoes
1 medium sweet onion (or 3 to 4 green onions)
salted macadamia nuts, finely crushed

Directions:

Peel the tomatoes (see "Tips"), cut them each in half, remove and discard seeds, *dice* the tomatoes, and place them in the mixing bowl. Slice the onions very thinly, and stir them into the tomatoes. Using your hands, shred the fish, and add it to the tomato mixture. Continue using your hands to "massage" the mixture. When it is thoroughly mixed together, cover with plastic wrap, and refrigerate until cold. Top with the macadamia nuts before serving.

Tips:

Serve this cold appetizer with crackers or bread.

Here's a trick that makes peeling tomatoes easy. Using the dullest edge of a butter knife, rub the entire tomato rather firmly. Then pull the skin off with a paring knife.

Hawaiian Tradition and History

Ancient rock paintings show that Hawaiian people have been surfing since first arriving on the Islands, yet missionaries had almost succeeded in completely wiping it out by 1890. A teenager named Duke Kahanamoku is credited with the return of surfing. Duke and some of his friends started a surfing club at Waikiki beach. They called their club *Hui Nalu*, which means "Club of the Waves," and they became known as the "Beach Boys of Waikiki."

Hawiian Food Tradition and History

If you were to fly over the Hawaiian Islands, you would probably notice hundreds of ponds (called *loko i'a*) along their shorelines. Some were built as long ago as A.D. 1200. Entire communities worked together to build many of these ponds, sometimes in just one night. The basic idea of the ponds was to allow small fish to swim into them through narrow slats. The fish were then fed things like breadfruit and taro. Eventually they grew too large to escape and were then harvested.

Quick–Fried Rice

Fried rice is a standard of Chinese cuisine. Make this recipe with meat or seafood and a wide assortment of vegetables for a quick and nutritious one-dish meal.

Ingredients:

6 cups cooked rice
3 eggs
2 tablespoons cooking oil
1 cup diced char siu (see page 45), ham, or shrimp
1½ cups diced cooked vegetables (peas, carrots, broccoli, etc.)
3 tablespoons soy sauce
1½ teaspoons sesame oil
salt to taste
4 tablespoons thinly sliced green onion

Taro and bamboo plants.

Cooking utensils you'll need:
measuring cups
measuring spoons
wire whisk
2 mixing bowls
wok or skillet

Directions:

Cook rice according to package directions. *Whisk* the eggs in one of the bowls, and set aside. Put the 2 tablespoons cooking oil in a hot wok, add the meat, stir-fry for about 30 seconds, and put the meat in one of the bowls. Pour the eggs into the wok, and scramble by stirring while cooking. Break the eggs into small pieces, and put them in the second bowl. Return meat to the wok, add cooked rice, and stir-fry for 2 minutes. Stir in vegetables, soy sauce, sesame oil, and eggs. Stir-fry 2 minutes, and add salt to taste. Sprinkle with sliced green onions, and serve.

Hawaiian Food Facts

Grilled fish of all types is a favorite food on the Islands. Hawaiians eat many fish that you may not have heard of, including: opakapaka, onaga, uku, ulua, aku, akule, ahi, kalekale, opihi, and wana. The Hawaiian state fish is the *humuhumunukunukuapua'a*! In English, that's the Picasso trigger fish.

Shrimp Tempura

Use tempura batter to add a tasty crunch to shrimp or vegetables.

Ingredients:

2 pounds medium shrimp
2 cups flour
1 cup cornstarch
¼ teaspoon salt
1 egg yolk
1 tablespoon cooking sherry
1 cup cold water
cooking oil

Cooking utensils you'll need:
measuring cups
measuring spoons
flour sifter
2 mixing bowls
wire whisk
candy thermometer
deep-sided pan for frying
plastic bag
long-handled slotted spoon

Directions:

Wash the shrimp. Do not remove the tails, but do remove the remainder of the shells and the black "veins." Make a shallow diagonal cut on the under-side of each shrimp, and set them aside. Sift 1 cup of flour, cornstarch, and salt into a mixing bowl, and set it aside. **Whisk** the egg yolk in the second mixing bowl, and stir in sherry and cold water. Pour about 3 inches of oil into the deep-sided pan, attach the thermometer, and heat the oil to 365°. Pour the egg mixture into the flour mixture, and stir. Put the remaining cup of flour into the plastic bag, add the shrimp, and shake to coat. Dip shrimp into the batter, place them on the slotted spoon, and carefully lower into the hot oil. **Deep-fry** the shrimp in batches, removing each one as it turns golden brown. Drain on paper towels to remove excess fat, and serve hot.

Tip:

Use this batter and method to deep-fry raw whole mushrooms, and broccoli and carrot slices. For dipping, serve soy sauce on the side.

Haupia

It only takes a few minutes to make this creamy coconut pudding. No wonder it's a staple dessert at Hawaiian luaus.

Ingredients:

6 tablespoons sugar
5 tablespoons cornstarch
2 cups canned coconut milk
1 cup whole milk

Cooking utensils you'll need:
measuring cups
measuring spoons
small mixing bowl
saucepan
individual serving dishes or 8-inch square pan

Directions:

Mix together sugar and cornstarch in the small bowl. Pour 1 cup coconut milk into the saucepan, and stir in the sugar/cornstarch mixture. Place the saucepan over low to medium heat, and cook, stirring constantly, until thickened. Stir in the remaining two types of milk, and continue cooking in the same manner until thickened. Pour into individual serving dishes or the square pan, and refrigerate until firm.

Tip:

Mandarin oranges or fresh fruit are pretty and refreshing garnishes for this pudding.

Hawaiian Food Tradition

You may be surprised to learn that the coconut tree is not native to the Hawaiian Islands, yet it is revered as a symbol of life. This tree is actually an "immigrant" to the Islands, like the Polynesian people who are responsible for bringing it there so many years ago. Although the coconut has been an important food source for many people, Hawaiians did not appreciate the tree for its food value nearly as much as for its other products. Every part of the tree came to be utilized in the Hawaiian culture. Coconut husks became food containers, leaves were used to make fans, and wood to make drums. Sennit, a rope fiber made from the husk, was used in the construction of canoes. The coconut tree also became an important symbol representing a link between the Hawaiian people, their ancestors, and god. According to the legend, Ku, the ancestor of the Hawaiian people, needed to return to the ancestral homeland but left his son behind. When the son told his mother how much he longed to be with his father, the mother sang, and a coconut tree sprouted and grew before her. The son began to climb the tree, the mother continued to sing, and the tree continued to grow and sway until it was so tall that it bent over and stretched all the way to Tahiti, forming a bridge between the islands.

Macadamia Nut Pie

Preheat oven to 325° Fahrenheit.

Ingredients:

3 eggs
⅔ cup sugar
1 cup light corn syrup
2 tablespoons melted butter
1 teaspoon vanilla
1½ cups chopped macadamia nuts
1 unbaked 9-inch pie shell

Cooking utensils you'll need:
measuring cups
measuring spoons
mixing bowl
electric mixer

Directions:

Put the eggs into the mixing bowl and beat well. Beat in the sugar, corn syrup, melted butter, and vanilla. Stir in the nuts, pour into the pie shell, and bake for 50 minutes (until the pie is *set*). Allow the pie to cool to room temperature, and then refrigerate.

Tip:

If you want to try making your own pie crust, mix ¾ cup flour with ¼ teaspoon salt. *Cut* in 2 tablespoons shortening. When the mixture looks like meal, cut in another 2 tablespoons shortening. Cut in 1½ tablespoons cold water. Gather the dough into a ball. Sprinkle flour on a flat surface, such as a wooden cutting board, and on a rolling pin. Place the dough on the flat surface, and pat it a little to begin flattening it out. Lift it up and put a little more flour under it. Begin rolling from the center outward and in all directions. Add more flour to the rolling pin as necessary. Lift up the edges of the dough and add more flour if necessary. When the dough is the size needed for the pie plate, fold it in half. Place the pie plate next to the dough, slide the dough into it, and open the folded dough up. Gently pat the dough into the pie plate, crimp the edges of the dough, and trim off any excess with a butter knife.

kanake' (kah nah KEH) - candy

Hawaiian Food History

A man named William Purvis introduced the macadamia, a native tree of Australia, to Hawaii in 1882. People wishing to grow macadamia nuts must be patient as it takes seven years from the time of planting before the tree will begin bearing nuts. The nuts must be allowed to ripen on the tree and are then picked by hand. July is the only month of the year when these hard-shelled nuts are not harvested. If you were to shell your own nuts, you would have to hit them with a hammer or a rock in order to reach the edible center. Demand for this delicacy far exceeds supply. That's why these uniquely flavored nuts are often quite expensive. Today, Hawaii is the largest grower of macadamia nuts in the world, producing ninety percent of the annual supply. Bees use the blossoms of macadamia nuts to produce a delicious honey.

Hawaiian Food History

Taro corms (tubers) are cooked and then pounded and mixed with water to make poi. At first, taro was steamed in underground fires. In later times, it was boiled over wood fires. Sometimes, children helped to pull the outer "skin" off of the boiled poi. After men pounded the poi, it was stored. Water could then be added before the poi was eaten. As early as the beginning of the twentieth century, poi was being marketed to places as far away as Vancouver, Canada. As you might expect, the process for commercial production is very efficient today. Modern poi mills can produce almost 200 pounds of poi per minute.

Poi Pudding

Make this pudding for dessert using the recipe below. If you would like to make a version for breakfast that is similar to porridge eaten by many children in Hawaii, see "Tip."

Ingredients:

⅓ cup whipping cream
2 tablespoons brown sugar, packed
dash of vanilla
⅓ cup poi
toasted coconut (optional)

Cooking utensils you'll need:
measuring cup
measuring spoon
mixing bowl
electric mixer
rubber spatula

Directions:

Whip the cream, brown sugar, and vanilla just to soft peaks. (Be careful not to over whip, or you will end up with sweetened buttermilk with little chunks of butter floating in it.) Use the rubber spatula to gently *fold* in poi. Refrigerate until ready to serve. Garnish servings with coconut, if desired.

Tip:

To make poi porridge for breakfast: Replace the whipping cream with 1/3 cup milk. Instead of whipping it, put the milk and sugar in a saucepan. Heat, stirring constantly, until it just begins to *simmer*. Stir in vanilla and poi. That's all there is to it. You might like to eat this warm porridge with fruit and toast.

Guava Banana Pie

Guava nectar is popular in Hawaii for both drinking and cooking. Here it's used to make a unique banana pie.

Ingredients:

1¼ cups guava nectar
½ cup sugar
1 tablespoon lemon juice
¼ teaspoon salt
3 tablespoons cornstarch
3 tablespoons cold water
1½ cups sliced bananas (Do not peel or slice until it is time to add bananas to the pie.)
1 baked 9–inch pie shell
one pint whipping cream
1 tablespoon confectioners' sugar (powdered sugar)

Cooking utensils you'll need:
measuring cups
measuring spoons
saucepan
small mixing bowl

Directions:

Bake the pie shell according to package directions. Pour the guava nectar into the saucepan. Stir in lemon juice, sugar, and salt. Place the pan over low heat, and bring the mixture to a boil. Meanwhile, put the cornstarch into the small bowl, and gradually stir in the water. Add the cornstarch mixture to the saucepan, and continue cooking until the pie filling has thickened, stirring constantly. Allow the filling to cool, peel and slice the bananas, and fold them into the filling. Pour the filling into the baked pie shell, cool to room temperature, and refrigerate. When ready to serve, whip the cream with the confectioners' sugar. Add a *dollop* of cream to each serving.

Tip:

If you would like to make your own pie shell, see "Tip" on pages 56–57. After placing the pie dough in the pie plate, prick the bottom in several places with a fork, and bake the pie shell at 450° degrees Fahrenheit for about 10 minutes or until done.

Hawaiian Food Facts

Although the guava tree is now common in many countries of the world, it probably did not arrive in Hawaii until the early nineteenth century. Guava fruit can be eaten fresh, but they have a strong odor that is eliminated by cooking. Guava nectar is popular in Hawaii for making ice cream sodas and punch.

Hawaiian Food Facts

Grenadine is a non-alcoholic syrup that is traditionally made from pomegranates. Because of the desirable climate in the Hawaiian Islands, many residents grow specimens of this 6-foot shrub in their yards. Pomegranates are one of the oldest known fruits. In fact, some people think that the "apple" spoken of in the story of Adam and Eve in the Garden of Eden was actually a pomegranate. Originally from the Middle East, this fruit probably arrived in North America with the Spanish conquistadors. French people were the first to make grenadine. Some grenadine that is sold today is made of citric acid combined with flavors and colors instead of pomegranates. So, if you want to be sure you have the real thing, you need to read the ingredients statement. You can try to make your own grenadine using real pomegranates. To do this, *simmer* the seeds (and their surrounding juice pouches) from a couple pomegranates in a small pan with just enough water to keep them from burning. Then put them in a piece of cheesecloth (or a sieve) and press them with a spoon to release the juice. Mix the juice with an equal amount of water, and simmer again for about 10 minutes. Be careful not to get pomegranate juice on your clothing because the resulting stains can be difficult to remove.

Pali Punch

Modern processing and shipping methods for fruit juices make it possible for you to mix this refreshingly fruity beverage no matter where you live.

Ingredients:

Two 46-ounce cans guava nectar
1½ cups unsweetened pineapple juice
1 cup orange juice
¾ cup lemon juice
¼ cup sugar
1 tablespoon grenadine syrup
1 bottle ginger ale
fresh fruit (see "Tip")

Cooking utensils you'll need:
measuring cups
measuring spoon
punch bowl or other large bowl
long-handled spoon

Directions:

Chill ginger ale and fruit juices for several hours prior to making the punch. Pour the guava nectar into the punch bowl, stir in the remaining ingredients, and serve.

Tip:

Use fresh fruit, such as thin slices of lemons and oranges, to garnish the punch. You can also put pieces of fruit, such as strawberries and pineapple chunks, into ice cube trays, cover them with water, and freeze. Add these fruit cubes to the punch bowl to keep the punch chilled.

Poi Cocktail

Poi, one of the most ancient Hawaiian foods, became available in some grocery stores in the middle of the twentieth century. Make this refreshing drink the next time you intend to have a hot and spicy meal, as milk helps to cool down one's mouth when eating hot peppers.

Cooking utensils you'll need:
measuring cups
measuring spoon
blender

Ingredients:

1 cup milk
¼ cup poi
½ teaspoon vanilla
crushed ice or ice cubes
cinnamon stick or ground nutmeg

Directions:

Put the milk, poi, and vanilla into the blender container. Add about 1 cup of crushed ice, and blend just until thick. Garnish with a cinnamon stick or sprinkle with nutmeg.

Tip:

If you wish to make a more savory version of this drink, eliminate vanilla, and instead add a sprinkle of sea salt (or kosher salt).

aloha

When Hawaiian people use this word they are saying much more than just hello or good bye. Aloha is like a blessing. It means "the presence of divine breath."

Hawaiian Food Facts

One cup of poi has just 120 calories. That's only half as much as rice! Vitamins C and B_1 are present in poi, along with iron, magnesium, potassium, and fiber. Interestingly, there is no word for indigestion in the Polynesian language. Some people say this is because the Polynesian diet relied heavily on poi, and the food is so easily digested that people did not experience indigestion. Taro, the source of poi, has been listed by the National Academy of Science as one of the world's most underutilized foods. Hawaiians make taro into chips as well as poi.

Further Reading

Alexander, Agnes. *How to Use Hawaiian Fruit*. Hilo, Hawaii: Petroglyph Press Ltd, 1999.

Carroll, Rick and Marcie Carroll (editors). *Traveler's Tales Hawai'i: True Stories of the Island Spirit*. San Francisco, Calif.: Travelers' Tales, Inc., 1999.

Kondo Corum, Ann. *Ethnic Foods of Hawaii*. Honolulu, Hawaii: Bess Press, 2000 (revised edition).

Laudan, Rachel. *The Food of Paradise: Exploring Hawaii's Culinary Heritage*. Honolulu, Hawaii: University of Hawaii Press, 1996.

Philpotts, Kaui. *Hawaiian Country Tables: Vintage Recipes for Today's Cooks*. Honolulu, Hawaii: Bess Press, 1998.

Riegert, Ray. *Hidden Big Island of Hawaii: Including the Kona Coast, Hilo, Kailua and Volcanos National Park*. Berkeley, Calif.: Ulysses Press, 2003.

Riegert, Ray. *Hidden Hawaii: Including Oahu, Maui, Kauai, Lanai, Molokai, and the Big Island*. Berkeley, Calif.: Ulysses Press, 2003 (12th edition).

Tong Parola, Shirley and Lisa Parola Gaynier. *Remembering Diamond Head, Remembering Hawai'i*. Shaker Heights, Ohio: Diamond Hawaii Press, 1999.

Wong, Alan. *Alan Wong's New Wave Luau: Recipes from Honolulu's Award-Winning Chef*. Berkeley, Calif.: Ten Speed Press, 2003.

Yamaguchi, Roy and John Harrisson. *Roy's Feasts from Hawaii*. Berkeley, Calif.: Ten Speed Press, 1995.

For More Information

Kitchen Safety
www.premiersystems.com/recipes/kitchen-safety/cooking-safety.html

Hawaii Historic Timeline
www.dcs-chico.com/~star/Hawaii/h_time.html

Hawaii History
http://www.hawaiischoolreports.com/history.htm

Hawaii Lei History
www.coffeetimes.com/leis.htm

Hawaii Marriage and Family
www.coffeetimes.com/marriage.html

Publisher's note:
The Web sites listed on this page were active at the time of publication. The publisher is not responsible for Web sites that have changed their addresses or discontinued operation since the date of publication. The publisher will review and update the Web sites upon each reprint.

Index

aloha 65

bananas 8, 21, 40, 41, 60
"Beach Boys of Waikiki" 49
beef 34, 36, 38
breadfruit 8, 21, 50

Char Siu Bao 45–47
Chicken Long Rice 43
chocolate 8
coconuts 8, 54, 55, 59
coffee 8
Committee of Safety 11
Cook, James 8
cotton 8

dairies 8
Dole, Sanford 11

family 22, 25, 29, 41
farms 11
fish 11, 13, 26, 36, 39, 48, 50, 52
food traditions 39

Gingered Carrots 28
grenadine 62, 63
guava 11, 60, 61, 63
Guava Banana Pie 60
hanai 29
Haupia 54
Hawaii, Kingdom of 11
Hawaii, U.S. territory 11
Hawaiian coleslaw 25
Hawaiian language 8
Hawaiian regional cuisine 11
Hoisin sauce 45, 47
hula 8

illegal overthrow of Hawaiian monarchy 11
"imu method" of cooking 41

Kalua Pig 40, 41
Kamaboko Salad 26
King David Kalakaua 8

leis 27

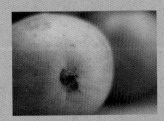

Loco Moco 36–37
Lomi Lomi 48
luau 25, 41, 43, 54
Lumpia and Sauce 38–39

Macadamia Nut Pie 56–57
macadamia nuts 18, 20, 21, 48, 56, 57
Malasadas 22–23
Mango Bread 20
mangoes 11, 20, 21
metric conversion table 14
missionaries 8, 34, 49

Pali Punch 63
papaya 21
patis 38, 39
pigs 8, 41
pineapples 8, 25
Pipi Kaula 34
plantations 8, 11, 39, 42
poi 11, 31, 33, 58, 59, 64, 65
Poi Cakes 31–32

Poi Cocktail 64
Poi Pudding 59
Polynesians 8, 33, 41, 55, 65
pomegranates 62
pomelo 21
ponds 50

Quick-Fried Rice 51

safety tips 12–13
sesame oil 11, 43, 45, 46, 51
Shrimp Tempura 53
soy sauce 11, 18, 34, 43, 45, 46, 51, 53
Spanish conquistadors 62
sugar cane 8
surfing 49

taro 8, 30, 31–33, 50, 58, 65
ti leaves 40, 41
tobacco 8

whaling 8

Author:

In addition to writing, Joyce Libal has worked as an editor for a half dozen magazines, including a brief stint as recipe editor at *Vegetarian Gourmet*. Most of her experience as a cook, however, has been gained as the mother of three children and occasional surrogate mother to several children from different countries and cultures. She is an avid gardener and especially enjoys cooking with fresh herbs and vegetables and with the abundant fresh fruit that her husband grows in the family orchard.

Consultant:

The Culinary Institute of America is considered the world's premier culinary college. It is a private, not-for-profit learning institution, dedicated to providing the world's best culinary education. Its campuses in New York and California provide learning environments that focus on excellence, leadership, professionalism, ethics, and respect for diversity. The institute embodies a passion for food with first-class cooking expertise.

Recipe Contributor:

Patricia Therrien has worked for several years with Harding House Publishing Service as a researcher and recipe consultant—but she has been experimenting with food and recipes for the past thirty years. Her expertise has enriched the lives of friends and family. Patty lives in western New York State with her family and numerous animals, including several horses, cats, and dogs.

Picture Credits